CIVIL WAR

CIVIL WAR

A LIBRARY OF CONGRESS BOOK

By MARTIN W. SANDLER

Introduction by James H. Billington, Librarian of Congress

HarperCollins*Publishers*

For Carol

ACKNOWLEDGMENTS

The author wishes to thank John Cole and Peggy Wagner of the Publishing Office of the Library of Congress for their help and support. Appreciation is expressed also to Liza Baker, Craig D'Oogie, the staff of the Prints and Photographs Division of the Library of Congress and Dennis Magnu of the Library's Photoduplication Service. As with all the books in this series, this volume and its author owe much to the guidance and editorial skill of Kate Morgan Jackson.

◆

Civil War
A Library of Congress Book

Library of Congress Cataloging-in-Publication Data
Sandler, Martin W.
Civil War / by Martin W. Sandler ; introduction by James H. Billington, Librarian of Congress.
p.   cm.
"A Library of Congress book."
ISBN 0-06-026024-6. — ISBN 0-06-026027-0 (lib bdg.)
1. United States—History—Civil War, 1861–1865—Pictorial Works—Juvenile Literature.
2. United States—History—Civil War, 1861–1865—Juvenile Literature.   1. United States—History—Civil War, 1861–1865.]
I. Title.
E468.7.S26   1996
973.7—dc20

95-1507
CIP
AC

Design by Tom Starace with Jennifer Abadi
1   2   3   4   5   6   7   8   9   10
❖
First Edition

Our type of democracy has depended upon and grown with knowledge gained through books and all the other various records of human memory and imagination. By their very nature, these records foster freedom and dignity. Historically they have been the companions of a responsible, democratic citizenry. They provide keys to the dynamism of our past and perhaps to our national competitiveness in the future. They link the record of yesterday with the possibilities of tomorrow.

One of our main purposes at the Library of Congress is to make the riches of the Library even more available to even wider circles of our multiethnic society. Thus we are proud to lend our name and resources to this series of children's books. We share Martin W. Sandler's goal of enriching our greatest natural resource—the minds and imaginations of our young people.

The scope and variety of Library of Congress print and visual materials contained in these books demonstrate that libraries are the starting places for the adventure of learning that can go on whatever one's vocation and location in life. They demonstrate that reading is an adventure like the one that is discovery itself. Being an American is not a patent of privilege but an invitation to adventure. We must go on discovering America.

James H. Billington
The Librarian of Congress

The Civil War was the most bitter conflict the United States has ever experienced. In less than five years, more than 600,000 young men were killed, hundreds of thousands of others were wounded, and half of the nation was laid in ruins. The war between the North and the South was also the most recorded conflict the world had ever known. From the moment it began, scores of artists and reporters took to the field, documenting every aspect of the war. They were joined on the battlefields and in the camps by a host of photographers using cameras and other equipment that had been invented less than ten years earlier. In the pages that follow, you will witness the scenes that these artists and photographers captured and will encounter the words of those caught up in a nation at war with itself.

Martin W. Sandler

A NATION DIVIDED

In 1860, the United States is a nation on the verge of war. It will be a conflict that pits two halves of the nation, North and South, against each other.

It will be a war unlike any the world has ever experienced. It will feature massive armies, fierce battles, extraordinary heroism and death and destruction on a scale almost too large to be fully understood.

A s in all wars, there are many reasons for the conflict. At the heart of the differences between the North and the South is the fact that the two great regions have developed in very different ways.

The South is primarily an agricultural area, with an economy based mainly on the growing of cotton. While the Northern landscape is filled with smoke-belching factories, the South has smoke-belching steamboats preparing to transport bales of cotton to the Northern factories and to manufacturers in Europe.

PREPARING FOR BATTLE!

The economic differences alone are not serious enough to cause a war. There are other factors. Raising and harvesting cotton requires an enormous number of field hands. The South meets this demand through the use of slave labor. On huge plantations and small farms throughout the South, approximately 4 million slaves, held against their will, form the labor force that sustains the cotton industry.

Slavery is an institution cruel beyond description. By the early 1800's, when the African slave trade is declared illegal, black men, women and children have already been captured on the continent and transported to the South in the stifling, overcrowded holds of wooden ships. Bound in chains, they are taken to auction houses and sold to the highest bidders. In the process, whole families are separated and are forced to enter a life without freedom.

God forgive us, but ours is a <u>monstrous</u> system, and wrong. . . .

—From the diary of Mary Chestnut,
a Southern woman, 1860

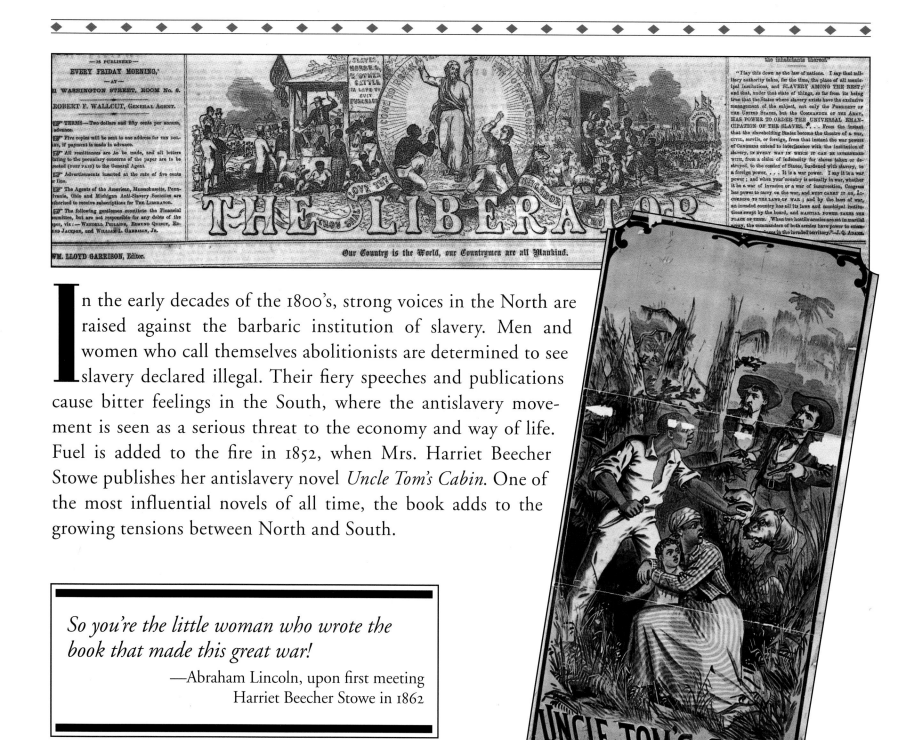

In the early decades of the 1800's, strong voices in the North are raised against the barbaric institution of slavery. Men and women who call themselves abolitionists are determined to see slavery declared illegal. Their fiery speeches and publications cause bitter feelings in the South, where the antislavery movement is seen as a serious threat to the economy and way of life. Fuel is added to the fire in 1852, when Mrs. Harriet Beecher Stowe publishes her antislavery novel *Uncle Tom's Cabin*. One of the most influential novels of all time, the book adds to the growing tensions between North and South.

So you're the little woman who wrote the book that made this great war!

—Abraham Lincoln, upon first meeting Harriet Beecher Stowe in 1862

UNCLE TOM'S CABIN
A.S. SEERS PRINT. (COPYRIGHTED)

She has gone,—she has left us in passion and pride,—
Our stormy-browed sister, so long at our side!
She has torn her own star from our firmament's glow,
And turned on her brother the face of a foe! . . .

—From the poem "Brother Jonathan's Lament for Sister Caroline," by Oliver Wendell Holmes, 1861

In 1859, tensions come to a head. Abolitionist John Brown attempts to start a slave revolt by leading a raid on the federal arsenal in Harpers Ferry, Virginia. Then, in 1860, Abraham Lincoln, whom Southerners see as a foe of slavery, is elected President of the United States.

President Abraham Lincoln

Upon news of Lincoln's election, seven Southern states secede from the United States and form the Confederate States of America. On April 12, 1861, forces of the newly forming Confederate army fire upon and capture the federal garrison at Fort Sumter, South Carolina. Four more Southern states then secede. The nation splits apart, and the North and South are at war.

The Civil War will test the loyalties of every family. Two brothers will be generals in the opposing armies. The commander of the Confederate navy will have a son killed in the Union navy. Three brothers of Mrs. Abraham Lincoln will die fighting for the South. Men who have been friends for years will find themselves opposing each other on the same bloody battlefield.

Union officers

Confederate officers

Almost all the generals, from both the North and South, previously served in the United States Army together. Robert E. Lee, the leader of the Confederate forces, assumes his duties after first being offered command of the Union forces. It is no wonder that the poet Walt Whitman will term the conflict "this strange, sad war."

We are coming, Father Abraham,
   three hundred thousand more,
From Mississippi's winding stream and
   from New England's shore;
We leave our ploughs and workshops,
   our wives and children dear,
With hearts too full for utterance,
   with but a single tear;
We dare not look behind us,
   but steadfastly before:
We are coming, Father Abraham,
   three hundred thousand more!

—From the song "We Are Coming, Father Abraham,"
by James Sloan Gibbons, 1861

The war begins with both sides confident of a quick victory. Men North and South are eager to join in the fray. In May of 1861, Abraham Lincoln's call for 500,000 volunteers is answered by the enlistment of 700,000. "It seems as if we were never alive 'til now, never had a country 'til now," writes a New York girl of the war fever the attack on Fort Sumter has touched off in the North.

The same confidence permeates the South. "All Mississippi is in a fever to get into the field," the governor of that state tells the Confederacy's president, Jefferson Davis. "So impatient did I become for starting," states a Southern volunteer, "that I felt like ten thousand pins were pricking me in every part of my body and started off a week in advance of my brothers."

We are a band of brothers,
*   and native to the soil,*
Fighting for the property we gained
*   by honest toil;*
And when our rights were threatened,
*   the cry rose near and far,*
Hurrah for the Bonnie Blue Flag that
*   bears a single star!*

Chorus:
Hurrah! Hurrah! for Southern Rights,
*   hurrah!*
Hurrah! for the Bonnie Blue Flag that
*   bears a single star!*

As long as the Union was faithful
*   to her trust,*
Like friends and like brothers we were
*   kind, we were just;*
But now when Northern treachery
*   attempts our rights to mar,*
We hoist on high the Bonnie Blue Flag
*   that bears a single star.*
—From the song "The Bonnie Blue Flag,"
by Harry Macarthy, 1861

Union soldiers and military supplies

To many observers, it appears that the North will win a quick, easy victory. The North has a much larger reservoir of manpower to draw upon—some 22 million people, as compared to a white population of 7 million in the South. While the South has about 18,000 manufacturing plants, the North contains more than 110,000 factories, most capable of turning out war supplies. Of the 31,256 miles of railroad in the United States, more than 22,000 are within Northern borders.

The North can make a steam engine, locomotive or railway car; hardly a yard of cloth or a pair of shoes can you make. You are rushing into war with one of the most powerful, ingeniously mechanical and determined people on earth—right at your doors. You are bound to fail.

—Future Northern general William T. Sherman to a Southern friend, Christmas Eve, 1860

The Confederates have their own advantages. The North will have to invade the South and fight on terrain familiar to the Southern forces. Cavalry will play an important role in the war, and Southerners brought up on farms and plantations are far better horsemen than most Northerners. The South will be commanded by Robert E. Lee, the greatest military strategist of the era, while the North will struggle throughout the war to find a commander with anything close to Lee's abilities. Perhaps the greatest advantage Southern soldiers will have is that they will be fighting to preserve their very way of life. This, more than anything, will be their greatest inspiration in waging war against the North, a foe with superior manpower and resources.

General Robert E. Lee

Southrons, hear your country call you!
Up, lest worse than death befall you!
To arms! To arms! To arms, in Dixie
Lo! all the beacon-fires are lighted,—
Let all hearts be now united!
To arms! To arms! To arms, in Dixie
Advance the flag of Dixie!
Hurrah! Hurrah!
For Dixie's land we take our stand,
And live or die for Dixie!
To arms! To arms!
And conquer peace for Dixie!
To arms! To arms!
And conquer peace for Dixie!

—From the song "Dixie,"
by Albert Pike, c.1860

A WAR WE'LL REMEMBER

The Civil War will be visually recorded in greater detail than any previous conflict. Included among the many illustrators will be such renowned artists as Winslow Homer, Edwin Forbes, Alfred R. Waud, Thomas Nast, Theodore Davis and Conrad Wise Chapman.

Long after the conflict is over, the scenes drawn by the artists will remain in the memories of men, women and children throughout the nation. "Oh these artists," exclaims a New York reporter. "They have brought the drama of this desperate struggle right to our firesides."

The Civil War will mark the first time in history that the full scope of a war is captured by the camera. Introduced in 1839, photography is still in its infancy when the struggle between the states erupts. Before the war is over, photographers, with their large, bulky cameras and huge glass plates, will become a familiar sight on battlefields and in camps throughout the war zones.

The most famous early American photographer is Mathew B. Brady. A successful studio photographer, Brady sees the Civil War as his opportunity to become the nation's first combat cameraman. He and the numerous photographers he hires, such as Timothy O'Sullivan, Alexander Gardner, George Barnard and George Cook, will capture thousands of images of a nation at war with itself. Brady's great contribution will be as an organizer, assembling the photographic teams, equipping them and sending them into the field.

Mathew B. Brady (at far right) with Union soldiers

A spirit in my feet said go, and I went.
—Mathew B. Brady,
speaking of photographing the Civil War, c. 1875

Union soldier

Confederate soldier

Union soldier

Before marching off with their units, many soldiers, North and South, will visit photographic studios to have portraits taken for the loved ones they are leaving behind.

Union soldiers

Union soldiers

These studio portraits and the photographic images that Brady and his cameramen take once the conflict begins will provide the nation with a permanent record of the men who took part in the tragedy of the Civil War.

W orking in difficult and often dangerous situations, Civil War photographers record the true face of war more vividly than has ever before been possible.

Many of the scenes recorded by the cameramen provide the most dramatic evidence that the war is being fought with the largest armies and the most equipment ever assembled.

More than anything else, the photographs give Americans, North and South, a true-to-life picture of the horror of armed conflict. "Mr. Brady," writes a New York reporter, "has done something to bring home to us the terrible reality and earnestness of war. . . . Crowds of people are constantly going up the stairs [of his gallery]. Follow them and you will find them bending over photographic views . . . taken immediately after the action."

SOLDIER BOYS

*Confederate
soldier*

As the artists and photographers compile their visual record of the conflict, their pictures reveal a startling fact: Hundreds of thousands of the men are not men at all—they are mere boys.

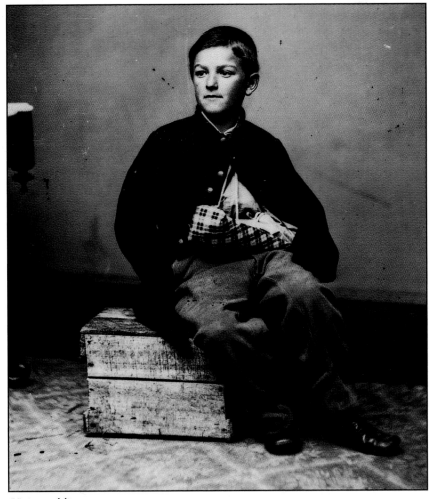

Union soldier

Before the Civil War is over, the Union army alone will include some 800,000 combatants under eighteen years old; over 200,000 under seventeen; and more than 100,000 under fifteen years of age.

Union soldier

> . . . *our hearts were touched with fire. It was given us to learn at the outset that life is a profound and passionate thing.*
> —From a letter written by former Union soldier Oliver Wendell Holmes, Jr., c. 1885

Left: Union sailor

Confederate artillery battery

Throughout the war, boys from both sides will run away from home to become soldiers or sailors. Patriotic parents will grant countless others permission to take part in the conflict. Some of the youngsters will become part of the artillery teams so important to both armies. Many will serve as drummer boys, whose job is to beat out the various military calls.

No matter how young they are, drummer boys often face great danger. They find themselves in the midst of battles, beating out the calls to charge or retreat. The history of the war is filled with stories of drummer boys who, in the heat of action, drop their drums to take up the guns of wounded soldiers and join in the fighting.

My mother said to me,
"You can do your part, my boy, for the land.
For if you will beat the drum,
you will take the place of a man."

—From the poem "The Drummer Boy,"
author unknown, c. 1862

FACE-TO-FACE

First Battle of Bull Run

With banners raised high, North and South march off to war, each convinced of a quick, glorious victory. They could not be more wrong. On July 21, 1861, in Manassas Junction, Virginia, at a stream called Bull Run, 30,000 Union troops come face-to-face with a large Confederate force.

All day long this first major battle of the Civil War rages. By late afternoon it seems that the Union forces will carry the day. But then the tide turns. Southern general Thomas "Stonewall" Jackson leads his troops in a brilliant stand. And when Confederate reinforcements arrive on the scene, the battle turns into a rout. The Union army makes a panicky, disorderly retreat toward Washington.

I saw a steady stream of men covered with mud, soaked through with rain . . . pouring irregularly, without any semblance of order, up Pennsylvania Avenue toward the Capitol. . . . I perceived they belonged to different regiments . . . mingled pell-mell together. . . . Hastily [I] . . . ran downstairs and asked an officer . . . where the men were coming from. "Where from? Well, sir, I guess we're all coming out of Virginny as far as we can, and pretty well whipped too. . . . I know I'm going home. I've had enough of fighting to last my lifetime.

—William Russell, an English journalist, encountering Northern troops coming from the First Battle of Bull Run, 1861

Left: First Battle of Bull Run

The casualty figures for this one encounter shock both sides. The North suffers 2,896 men killed, wounded or missing. Southern losses come to 1,982. What no one can foresee is that these figures are modest compared to battles still to come.

Confederate soldier

Second Battle of Bull Run

Because of this shocking encounter, the names Bull Run and Manassas Junction (the name given to the same battle by Southerners) will become famous in American military history. Later in the war, another fierce engagement will take place on the very same spot. But it is the First Battle of Bull Run that will lead a Union general to remind the nation that "War means fighting and fighting means dying."

The Civil War is fought very differently from twentieth-century wars. In an age of limited communications and transportation, there are often long breaks between battles. During these interludes, the battle zones become filled with huge camps where the armies live, drill and await the next call to arms.

Here, on a large plain, surrounded by an amphitheater of bluffs, were collected about 70,000 of our troops, presenting from the high ground a most magnificent sight. On all sides but the north there were tents,—high marquees for the officers, and low shelter-tents for the men. To the northward was the river with its gunboats. . . . In every other direction . . . there was a solid mass of tents and artillery and wagons, extending to a great distance. Twenty square miles were . . . covered by that camp. . . .

—From the diary of a Union soldier, 1863

CAMP LIFE

The First Battle of Bull Run makes it clear that the war cannot be won with untrained recruits. Each camp becomes a training site where officers spend long hours drilling their men on battle strategies and techniques. "The first thing in the morning we drill," writes a Union soldier. "Then we drill some more. Between drills we drill again."

The camps are packed with the tents in which the soldiers live. The standard tent, housing five or six men, is called the "A" because of its shape. Outside the tents the men receive their meals, which are cooked over open fires.

The boys say that our "grub" is enough to make a mule desert, and a hog wish he had never been born.

—Letter from a Union soldier

During winter months, walls made of long logs are stockaded around the tents. Chimneys are erected so that fires can be built inside the tents to keep the soldiers warm. Few nineteenth-century battles are fought in winter. Life in the camps during this waiting period becomes terribly boring. "Oh how tiresome this camp life [is] to me," a Confederate boy complains, "one everlasting monotone, yesterday, today and tomorrow."

The challenge of daily camp life in any season is to find ways to relieve the boredom between battles. Carrying out simple chores like doing one's laundry, preparing a meal, cutting firewood or writing letters back home helps break the monotony.

Photographers, eager to record every aspect of the war, are present in almost every camp. Clowning for their cameras provides another outlet from the dull routine of camp life.

Gambling is the most common escape from boredom. Men in both armies bet on everything from horse races to card games and dominoes. In many camps, money is wagered on cockfights, one of the most popular sports of the day.

Last Saturday a very exciting contest came off between two blooded horses, owned by two Brigadier Generals. Another match is announced for tomorrow and another for Saturday. With such examples, is it any wonder that gambling is on the increase? So far as my observation goes, nine men of every ten play cards for money.

—Letter from a Union soldier, 1864

The emotions raised by the Civil War inspire hundreds of songs. Many of these songs, sung around campfires by soldiers from both armies, tell of experiences shared a long way from home.

We're tenting tonight on the
old camp ground,
Give us a song to cheer
Our weary hearts, a song of home,
And friends we love so dear.
Many are the hearts that are
weary tonight,
Wishing for the war to cease;
Many are the hearts that are
looking for the right,
To see the dawn of peace.
Tenting tonight, tenting tonight,
Tenting on the old
camp ground.

—From the song "Tenting Tonight on the
Old Camp Grounds,"
by Walter Kittredge, c. 1862

Song sheet cover: "Our Country and Flag"

Other songs relate the feelings of men separated from those they love. The majority of Civil War songs from both sides of the conflict are written to arouse patriotic feelings. Ironically, the most popular Northern song, "The Battle Hymn of the Republic," is based on a Southern hymn, while the most popular Confederate song, "Dixie," is borrowed from a Northern minstrel tune.

Yes, we'll rally round the flag, boys,
    we'll rally once again,
    Shouting the battle cry of Freedom,
We will rally from the hillside,
    we'll gather from the plain,
Shouting the battle cry of Freedom.

Chorus:
    The Union forever, hurrah! boys, hurrah!
    Down with the traitor, up with the star,

    While we rally round the flag, boys,
    Rally once again,
    Shouting the battle cry of Freedom.
    —From the song "The Battle Cry of Freedom,"
    by George Frederick Root, c.1860

Song sheet cover:
"The Soldier's Dream of Home"

ON LAND AND ON SEA

Union gunboat Cairo

The Civil War is also fought on the sea, and most of the sea power belongs to the North. By the war's end, the Union navy will include 670 ships manned by 51,000 sailors and officers, whereas the Confederate navy will have 130 ships and 4,000 men. Soon after the fall of Fort Sumter, Abraham Lincoln orders a naval blockade of the South. In response, the South rebuilds a steam frigate, the *Merrimac,* and covers it with 4-inch iron plate. On March 8, 1862, the South's renovated ironclad, renamed the *Virginia,* appears on the scene and quickly puts several Northern ships out of action. On the next day, the Union navy sends its first iron-coated vessel, the *Monitor,* to do battle with the *Virginia.* The first clash of ironclads in history lasts five hours, with neither ship able to sink the other.

Though both sides begin to produce ironclad ships in greater numbers, the North's greater ship building facilities will allow the Union to construct far more iron-plated vessels than the Confederacy. Throughout the war, the North's blockade strategy will be bolstered by these new monsters at sea.

The War Between the States produces many naval heroes. One of the greatest is the South's Captain Robert B. Pegram, who time and again will slip his vessel, the *Nashville,* through Northern blockades to deliver munitions for Confederate troops. Union admiral David G. Farragut makes his mark at the Battle of Mobile Bay against Southern blockade runners. He climbs onto the rigging of his wooden flagship and utters one of the most famous commands in all naval history: "Damn the torpedoes!" Farragut cries. "Full speed ahead."

Admiral Farragut at Mobile Bay

The Confederacy was not [only] shot to death. It was strangled to death.
—Letter from a Civil War observer, 1865

Left: Battle between the Monitor *and the* Virginia

Union dead at Antietam

Battle of Antietam

While the Union navy focuses on strengthening its blockade and the Confederates struggle to keep their ports open, the war on land rages on. In the year following the First Battle of Bull Run, several battles are fought, resulting in heavy casualties on both sides. On September 17, 1862, the armies meet at Antietam Creek, near the village of Sharpsburg, Maryland. During the Battle of Antietam, Confederate commander Robert E. Lee brilliantly outmaneuvers his enemy but is forced to withdraw because of the superior number of Northern troops. The Union commander, General George McClellan, however, fails to follow up his advantage by pursuing Lee. The Battle of Antietam results in the bloodiest single day of the entire war, with almost 24,000 men killed or wounded in the battle.

As soon as the guns fall silent at Antietam, Abraham Lincoln travels to the battlefield for a confrontation with General George McClellan. The President is outraged by the Union commander's failure to move more boldly against the South. Soon he will replace McClellan with another commander. In his attempt to find someone who will lead decisively, he will appoint eight different generals to the post of commander.

Abraham Lincoln at Antietam

We had them within our grasp. We had only to stretch forth our hands and they were ours. And nothing I could say or do could make the Army move.

—President Abraham Lincoln, 1862

While the Battle of Antietam fails to produce the decisive victory that Abraham Lincoln has been waiting for, the Union's success gives him the opportunity to take action. Within a week of Antietam, the President issues his historic Emancipation Proclamation, declaring formally to the world that all slaves in areas still in rebellion on January 1, 1863, would be "then, thenceforeward, and forever free." For Northerners, what had started as a war to save the Union now becomes a conflict that, if victorious, will free the slaves.

Provost Guard of the 107th Colored Infantry at Fort Corcoran, part of the

Once let the black man get upon his person the brass letter, <u>U.S.</u>; let him get an eagle on his button, and a musket on his shoulder and bullets in his pocket, and there is no power on earth which can deny that he has earned the right to citizenship in the United States.
—From a speech by Frederick Douglass, 1861

From the moment that the first shots of the war are fired, abolitionists urge the enlistment of African Americans into the Union army. However, it is not until after the Emancipation Proclamation is issued that the recruitment of African Americans begins. More than 180,000 black soldiers and thousands of black sailors will join in the struggle. Many will be assigned menial tasks, and all will be commanded by white officers. But thousands of African Americans will engage in combat, and more than 40,000 will give their lives in the struggle that has such special meaning for them.

Battle of Fort Wagner

It is not too much to say that if this Massachusetts 54th had faltered when its trial came, two hundred thousand troops for whom it was a pioneer would never have put into the field. . . . But it did not falter. It made Fort Wagner such a name for the colored race as Bunker Hill had been for ninety years to the white Yankees.

—*New York Tribune,* 1863

Typical of the extraordinary bravery displayed by African-American combat troops is the valor shown by the all-black Massachusetts 54th. On July 18, 1863, as part of the Union campaign to capture Charleston, South Carolina, 600 men of the 54th attack the Confederate stronghold of Fort Wagner. More than forty percent of the troops die in the assault. When the division's color bearer is killed, Sergeant William Carney picks up the flag and, despite bullets in his leg, arm, and chest, proudly carries it back to his lines. For his actions he will receive the Congressional Medal of Honor, becoming the first of twenty-three African Americans to earn the nation's highest military award during the war.

A MODERN WAR

The Civil War is the world's first modern conflict. It introduces new methods and tools of warfare: mass armies, enormous guns, hand grenades, flame projectors, armored ships, torpedoes, trench warfare, aerial observation balloons, the telegraph and the railroad. The rifles carried by both Northern and Southern soldiers have been made more deadly than ever before. They can kill at a distance of half a mile and can deliver two or three shots a minute. The various cannons introduced in the war are the deadliest weapons of all. They can shoot farther, and cause more destruction, than any artillery pieces ever used.

One of the most fearsome of all the artillery pieces developed during the war is the 17,120-pound mortar gun called the Dictator. Built to fire a shell weighing 200 pounds, the gun is so heavy that it has to be transported along a railway track. In the latter stages of the war, it will be used effectively by Union forces during the siege of Petersburg, Virginia, where it will propel its enormous shells over 2.7 miles into the city.

The bursting of the shell [in Petersburg] was . . . terrific, an immense crater being formed in the ground where it fell, and earth, stones, and sod being scattered in every direction, much to the [horror] of the inhabitants of the place.

—Photographer Alexander Gardner, 1864

The Civil War introduces new military strategies as well as new weapons. The increased accuracy of rifles and the introduction of trench warfare diminishes the use of the close-order infantry charge. Still, in many battles huge waves of Union and Confederate soldiers attack each other in a straight line, moving ever forward and closing ranks as fellow infantrymen are killed or wounded.

There were, [within] a few feet of us . . . seventy-nine North Carolinians laying [sic] *dead in a straight line. I stood on their right and looked down their line. It was perfectly dressed. Three had fallen to the front, the rest had fallen backward: yet the feet of all these dead men were in a perfectly straight line.*

—Confederate artilleryman, 1863

uch lighter artillery pieces also cause incredible destruction. Efficient and easily movable, they become a major weapon in almost every land battle of the war.

New methods of fighting on the sea, as well as on land, are introduced. As armor-covered vessels replace sail-driven men-of-war, stationary cannons give way to guns placed on revolving turrets. Able to fire in any direction, the ironclads become increasingly efficient fighting machines.

Everything the finger of [this] war touches is revolutionized.

—*New York Herald,* 1861

In 1844, fourteen years before the Civil War began, Samuel Morse perfected the telegraph. The conflict between the states marks the first time that this extraordinary invention is put to use during wartime. Wherever the troops move, their telegraph corps erects the poles and strings the lines that make communications within an army faster and easier than ever before.

Although the invention of the airplane is still some forty years away, the Civil War is fought from the air as well as the land and sea. Men, carried aloft by huge observation balloons, take to the sky to report enemy troop movements and battle strategies.

Union soldiers stringing telegraph lines

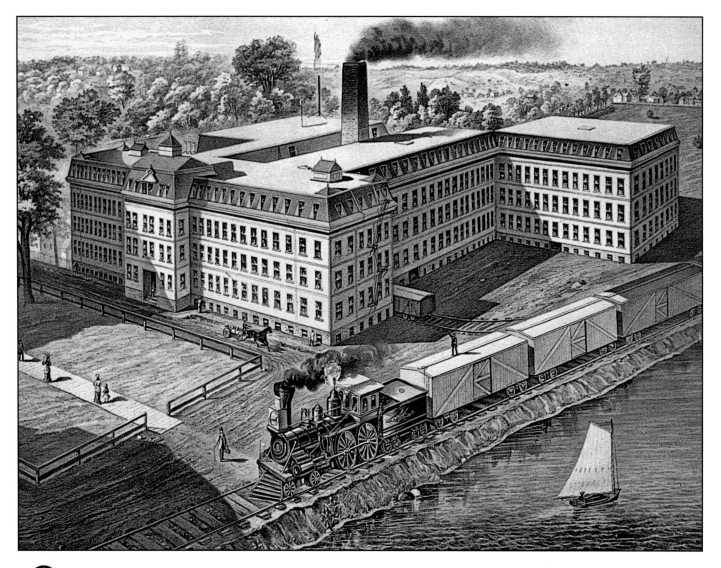

Of all the new developments of the first half of the 1800's, it is the railroad that most profoundly changes Americans' way of life. Development of the railroad in the North is far greater than that in the South. Throughout the war, the Northern railroad system plays a vital role in moving troops and weapons with speed and efficiency.

The Union's Corps of Engineers performs a key function by repairing tracks destroyed by the Confederates and by erecting enormous bridges, enabling military trains to cross even the most challenging terrain.

A s deadly as Civil War battles are, the greatest number of deaths in the conflict come not from bullets or cannonballs but from disease and inadequate medical treatment.

F ew medical people are aware that a surgeon's hands must be washed before an operation and that surgical dressings need to be sterilized. Tens of thousands of captured Union and Confederate soldiers die from illness or from their wounds in military prisons, where treatment is especially primitive.

As the Civil War progresses, women play increasingly important roles. Dr. Elizabeth Blackwell, the first woman to graduate from medical school, organizes a training program for Union nurses. Women, North and South, serve as nurses at military hospitals both in the field and behind the lines. Clara Barton, who will later found the American Red Cross, works tirelessly to send medical supplies to the sick and wounded. Women wrap bandages and collect books, toilet articles and other supplies to send to the troops. In both North and South, tens of thousands of women operate farms and work at other jobs, replacing the men who have gone off to war.

Several women on each side of the conflict play a dangerous role in the war, serving as spies. The most well known is Mrs. Rose O'Neil Greenhow, a Southern sympathizer who lives in Washington when the war breaks out. In the early stages of the war she learns of Union troop movements and sends this information to Southern generals at the front. Her actions are eventually discovered, and she is arrested and placed in a federal prison. It is later discovered that even while in jail, she is able to gather information and pass it on to Confederate officers.

TURNING POINTS

General Ulysses S. Grant at the Battle of Vicksburg

There are events in almost every war that can later be regarded as major turning points. In the first days of July 1863, two such events take place. For months, Northern land and naval forces have been attempting to capture the city of Vicksburg, Mississippi, the last Southern stronghold on the vital Mississippi River. Spirited attacks on the city by Northern general Ulysses S. Grant have resulted in five Union victories, but still the Confederates hold on. Grant decides that the city can be taken only by siege. For six days, Union ships and troops ring the city so tightly that, in the words of a Confederate soldier, "a cat could not have crept out of Vicksburg without being discovered." Finally, with his food and munitions almost gone, Southern general John C. Pemberton surrenders the city to Grant.

*Gettysburg on the eve
of the battle*

Three days before the events at Vicksburg come to a close, hundreds of miles to the north and east, in Gettysburg, Pennsylvania, the most important battle of the war is about to take place. Like many of this war's military engagements, it will be waged in a quiet, peaceful town whose name will join the ranks of the world's most famous military locales.

Left: Battle of Vicksburg

Battle of Gettysburg

The Battle of Gettysburg takes place by accident. General Robert E. Lee, determined to invade the North and win a victory important for Southern morale, leads his army toward Harrisburg, Pennsylvania, where he hopes to destroy railroad bridges linking East with West. He is unaware that a large Union force headed by General Meade is headed in the same direction. On July 1, 1863, the two forces come together, and a devastating battle begins.

Lucid, pure, and calm and blameless
*   Dawned on Gettysburg the day*
That should make the spot, once fameless,
*   Known to nations far away.*
Birds were caroling, and farmers
*   Gladdened o'er their garnered hay,*
When the clank of gathering armors
*   Broke the morning's peaceful sway. . . .*
—From the poem "Gettysburg: A Battle Ode," by
George Parsons Lathrop, 1863

The Battle of Gettysburg lasts for three days. On the first day of battle, the Confederates are victorious, but on the second day, Lee's attempts to encircle Meade's forces are beaten back. On the third day, Lee orders a direct assault across the valley separating the armies. Though they fight with extraordinary courage, the Confederates suffer a major defeat. The combined casualties for both sides are enormous: more than 7,000 killed and 44,000 wounded.

Slowly, over the misty fields of Gettysburg . . . came the sunless morn, after the retreat by Lee's broken army. Through the shadowy vapors, it was, indeed, a "harvest of death" that was presented. . . . Such a picture conveys a useful moral: . . . Here are the dreadful details! Let them aid in preventing such another calamity falling upon the nation.

—Photographer Alexander Gardner, 1863

The Battle of Gettysburg ends the Confederate army's sole offensive thrust into Union territory. Ending on the same day as the Southern defeat at Vicksburg, Gettysburg is a blow from which the Confederacy never recovers.

Some five months after the pivotal battle, Abraham Lincoln journeys to Gettysburg to dedicate the field of battle as a cemetery containing the graves of the Northern and Southern soldiers who died in the battle. In ten sentences, the eloquent Lincoln, president of a nation torn apart, delivers the most memorable speech in all of American history.

. . . we cannot dedicate—we cannot consecrate—we cannot hallow—this ground. The brave men, living and dead, who struggled here have consecrated it far above our poor power to add or detract. The world will little note, nor long remember, what we say here, but it can never forget what they did here.

—From Abraham Lincoln's Gettysburg Address,
November 19, 1863

As the third year of the bitter struggle grinds to an end, the abundance of resources produced in the North begins to take its toll. While three years of fighting have seriously diminished Confederate supplies, ranging from shoes and uniforms to guns and ammunition, Northern factories continue to produce enormous quantities of arms and munitions. River docks throughout military areas become crammed with Union reinforcements and weapons headed for the front lines.

Grant has a railroad of his own, a sure-enough iron rail, all the way from City Point, around by the east and south of Petersburg, along the line that his army occupies. So vast are the resources and appliances of war at his command. They do not spare in means or men, but are lavish of both.

—Confederate soldier, 1864

Northern reinforcements

Southern supplies become so scarce that, in some places along the front, Southern artillery batteries, short of weapons, disguise logs as cannons, hoping to deceive Northern scouts. But nothing can keep the caravans of Northern men and equipment from rolling to the front. To many observers, North and South, it begins to appear that nothing can overcome the seemingly unlimited resources that the Union is willing to throw into the fray.

I had no shoes. I tried it barefoot, but somehow my feet wouldn't callous [sic]. They just kept bleeding. I found it so hard to keep up that though I had the heart of a patriot, I began to feel I didn't have patriotic feet. Of course, I could have crawled on my hands and knees, but then my hands would have got so sore I couldn't have fired my rifle.

—Confederate soldier,
explaining his absence from a battle, 1864

Northern supply caravan

Union victories at Vicksburg and Gettysburg finally give President Abraham Lincoln something to cheer about, and most importantly, he at last finds a general willing to engage and pursue the enemy. Ulysses S. Grant's spirited actions at Vicksburg and in other battles in the West convince Lincoln that he is the man who can finally lead the Union to victory. In May of 1864, the president names Grant general in chief of the Union armies.

General Ulysses S. Grant

General Grant is not without his detractors, many of whom complain that he drinks too much. Lincoln responds by stating that if he can find out where Grant gets his whiskey, he will send the same brand to all the Union generals. "I cannot spare this man," says Lincoln. "He fights."

L incoln has found in Ulysses S. Grant a commander who, far more than any of his other generals, understands the nature of the Union's advantages. Grant knows that the only way to defeat the Southern army, so brilliantly led but increasingly short of resources, is to keep attacking no matter what the cost.

Battle of the Wilderness

Both sides are growing tired. Were it left solely and exclusively to the men in the two armies, I believe peace would be made before Christmas.

—Confederate soldier, 1864

O n May 4, 1864, between the Rapidan River and the village of Spotsylvania, Virginia, in an area called the Wilderness, Grant launches this relentless new strategy. The three-day Battle of the Wilderness does not result in victory for either side, but Robert E. Lee's troops suffer some 10,000 casualties that the Confederate army cannot afford.

As part of Grant's strategy for bringing the South to its knees, Union general William Tecumseh Sherman is ordered to march the huge forces under his command, from Chattanooga, Tennessee, through Georgia all the way to the Atlantic Coast. He is instructed to destroy everything in his path, including private houses, crops, factories, warehouses, bridges, railroads and public buildings. It is a cruel strategy designed to bring an end to a cruel war. As they march through Georgia, Sherman's troops cut a swath of devastation three hundred miles long and sixty miles wide. The destruction and loss of life that the general and his army cause will haunt Sherman for the rest of his life.

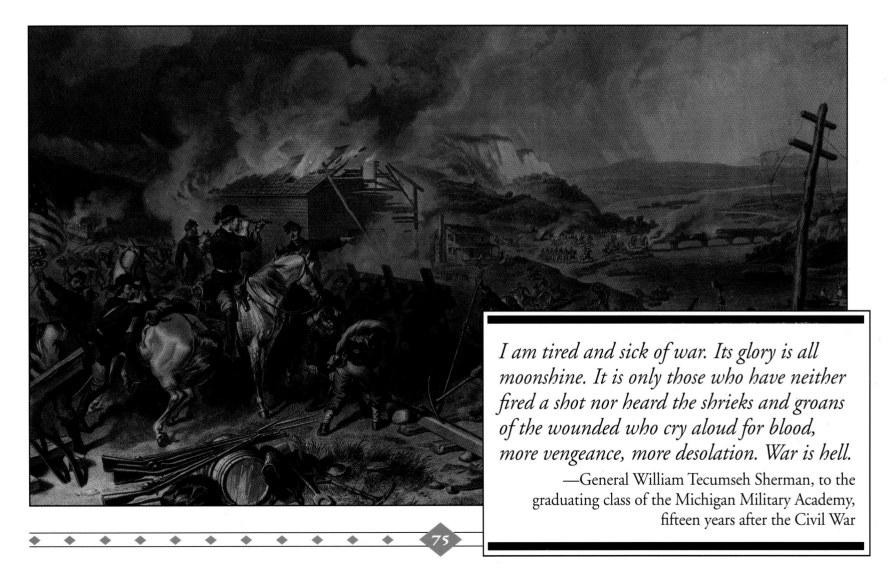

I am tired and sick of war. Its glory is all moonshine. It is only those who have neither fired a shot nor heard the shrieks and groans of the wounded who cry aloud for blood, more vengeance, more desolation. War is hell.

—General William Tecumseh Sherman, to the graduating class of the Michigan Military Academy, fifteen years after the Civil War

As the year 1865 begins, the end of the Confederate rebellion is close at hand. The capture by Union forces of Fort Fisher in North Carolina on January 15 strengthens the naval blockade of the South and spreads hunger throughout its civilian population. On April 1, Lee makes what will be his final assault of the war at Five Forks, Virginia, but is repelled. After four long years, Lee has run out of strategies and is almost out of men.

Capture of Fort Fisher

Battle of Five Forks

Nearly every major campaign of the war has been waged on Southern territory. By the time Sherman completes his march to the sea, much of this once-prosperous part of the nation is in ruins. Thousands of civilians are forced to flee to avoid Union naval bombardments and the ever-advancing Northern armies.

Ruins at Richmond

Citizens fleeing Richmond

By the end of the conflict, most of the great cities of the South are destroyed. Richmond, Virginia; Charleston and Columbia, South Carolina; Atlanta, Georgia; Jackson, Mississippi, and others lie in ashes. A Northern observer writes upon entering a Southern city, "It is now a wilderness of ruins. Its heart is but a mass of blackened chimneys and crumbling walls. Two thirds of the buildings in this place were burned, including, without exception, everything in the business portion."

On our part not a sound of trumpet more, nor roll of drum; not a cheer . . . but an awed stillness rather, and breath-holding, as if it were the passing of the dead! As each successive division halts, the men face inward toward us across the road, twelve feet away; then carefully "dress" their line. . . . They fix bayonets, stack arms; then, hesitatingly, remove cartridge-boxes and lay them down. Lastly . . . they tenderly fold their flags, battle-worn and torn, blood-stained, heart-holding colors, and lay them down; some frenziedly rushing from the ranks . . . pressing them to their lips with burning tears. And only the Flag of the Union greets the sky!

—Union general Joshua L. Chamberlain, in a letter describing the surrender of Confederate troops at Appomattox Courthouse, 1865

With his once-mighty army now reduced to some 25,000 men and all escape routes blocked, Robert E. Lee realizes that his only option is to surrender. On April 9, 1865, at Appomattox Courthouse, Virginia, Lee meets with Grant and surrenders his troops. Grant, in turn, graciously agrees "to let all the men who claim to own a horse or mule take the animals home with them to work their little farms." The War Between the States is finally over.

On May 24, 1865, the victorious Union armies parade triumphantly down Washington's Pennsylvania Avenue. It is not an exuberant parade. The mood of both the army and the nation is one of enormous relief. So many have died, so much has been destroyed, so much needs to be done to put the United States back together, that there is little call for jubilation. "How could we help falling on our knees," states a Union officer, "all of us together, and praying to God to pity and forgive us all."

When Johnny comes marching home again,
   Hurrah! Hurrah!
We'll give him a hearty welcome then,
   Hurrah! Hurrah!
The men will cheer, the boys will shout,
The ladies they will all turn out,
   And we'll all feel gay,
When Johnny comes marching home.
—From the song "When Johnny Comes Marching Home," by Patrick Sarsfield Gilmore, 1863

The final casualty figures for the war reveal the catastrophic toll the conflict has exacted. Approximately 360,000 Union soldiers and more than 260,000 Confederates have lost their lives. In addition, more than 275,000 Northern soldiers and some 100,000 Confederates have been wounded.

President Abraham Lincoln, 1860

The anguish of the conflict is perhaps most clearly etched on the face of Abraham Lincoln, the man who has borne the burden of leading his nation during its most tragic experience. Five days after the surrender treaty is signed, Lincoln is assassinated by a Southern sympathizer. The man who will come to be known as the Great Emancipator is the last great casualty of the war.

President Abraham Lincoln, 1865

O Captain! my Captain! our fearful trip is done,
The ship has weather'd every rack, the prize we sought is won,
The port is near, the bells I hear, the people all exulting,
While follow eyes the steady keel, the vessel grim and daring;
    But O heart! heart! heart!
        O the bleeding drips of red,
            Where on the deck my Captain lies
                Fallen cold and dead.

—From the poem "O Captain!
My Captain!" by Walt Whitman

ROAD TO RECONCILIATION

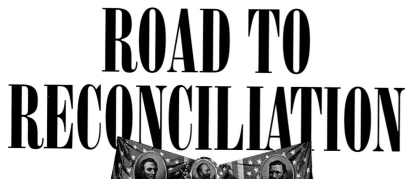

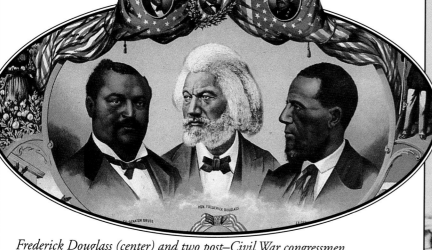

Frederick Douglass (center) and two post–Civil War congressmen

Tasks as challenging as the waging of the war itself lie ahead of the nation. The South must be almost entirely rebuilt. Bitter enemies, North and South, must be reconciled. Millions of ex-slaves, for generations denied freedom and education, must find a place in American society. Great African Americans will emerge as leaders in the fight for equality, but their struggles for rights and opportunities for all African Americans will be long and difficult and will not be fully realized even today.

Song sheet cover: "The Battle of Shiloh"

In the years following the war, almost every town, North and South, will erect a monument commemorating the Civil War and honoring the soldiers it sent off to battle. Hundreds of novels, short stories and histories will be written about the struggle. Through these writings and through countless songs, movies and other remembrances, the names of battlefields like Shiloh, Antietam, Gettysburg, Chancellorsville and Chickamauga will become enshrined in the history of the nation.

B ut it is the men who fought the battles who are most remembered. Their courage and their sacrifices will never be forgotten. Through them, the United States survived its greatest test, fulfilling Abraham Lincoln's immortal words, "that government of the people, by the people, and for the people, shall not perish from the earth."

The Library of Congress

All of the photographs, lithographs, engravings, paintings, line drawings, posters, song lyrics, song-sheet covers, and other illustrative materials contained in this book have been culled from the collections of the Library of Congress. The Library houses the largest collection of stored knowledge on earth. Within its walls lie treasures that show us how much more than a "library" a great library can be.

The statistics that help define the Library are truly amazing. It has more books from America and England than anywhere else, yet barely one half of its collections are in English. It contains more maps, globes, charts and atlases than any other place on earth. It houses one of the largest collections of photographs in the world, the largest collection of films in America, almost every phonograph record ever made in the United States and the collections of the American Folklife Center. The Library also contains over six million volumes on hard sciences and applied technology.

It is a very modern institution as well. Dr. James Billington, the Librarian of Congress, has defined the Library's future through his vision of a "library without walls." "I see the Library of Congress in the future," he has said, "as an active catalyst for civilization, not just a passive mausoleum of cultural accomplishments of the past." A good example of this commitment is the Library's National Demonstration Laboratory, which, through hands-on work stations, offers over 200 examples of the latest innovations in interactive video and computer learning.

The Library of Congress was originally established to serve the members of Congress. Over the years it has evolved into a great national library. Unlike almost every other national library in the world, the Library of Congress does not limit the use of its collections to accredited scholars. Ours is a national library made by the people for the people, and is open to all the people. Fondly referred to as "the storehouse of the national memory," it is truly one of our proudest and most important possessions.

Index

Numbers in *italics* indicate photographs and illustrations.

Abolitionists
and African American enlistment, 52
and antislavery movement, 14, 15
African Americans, *52, 82*
and slave trade, 12, *12,* 13, *13*
as soldiers, 52, *52,* 53
after the war, 82, *82*
agriculture, in the South, 11, 12, *12*
Antietam, Battle of, 50, *50,* 51, 83
Appomattox Courthouse, Virginia, 78
arms and ammunition
and blockade runners, 49
modern technology of, 54, 56
supplies of, 71, 72
artillery, *28*
and modern warfare, 54, *54,* 55, *55,* 57, *57*
and young soldiers, 32
artists, and Civil War, 22, 23
See also photography
Atlanta, Georgia, 77

Barnard, George, 25
Barton, Clara, 64
"Battle Cry of Freedom, The" (song), 47

"Battle Hymn of the Republic, The", 47
Blackwell, Elizabeth, 64
blockade runners, 49
"Bonnie Blue Flag, The" (song), 19
Brady, Mathew B., 25, *25,* 27, 29
Bull Run, First Battle of, *34,* 34–37, *35,* 40
Bull Run, Second Battle of, 37, *37*

Camp life, 38–39, *38–39*
and boredom, 42, 43, 44
and food, 41
and gambling, 45, *45*
tents for, 41, *41,* 42, *42*
in winter, 42, *42*
cannons. *See* artillery
Carney, William, 53
casualties, medical treatment of, 62, 63, *62–63,*
64–65
casualty figures, 7, 80, 81
for African Americans, 52
at Antietam, 50
at Battle of the Wilderness, 74
at First Battle of Bull Run, 36
at Fort Wagner, 53

at Gettysburg, 69
cavalry, role of, 21
Chamberlain, Joshua L., 78
Chancellorsville, Battle of, 83
Chapman, Conrad Wise, 22
Charleston, South Carolina, 53, 77
Chickamauga, Battle of, 83
cockfighting, and camp life, 45, *45*
communications, in the field, 38, 54, 59, *59*
Confederate Army, *17, 19*
age of soldiers in, 30, *30,* 32, *32,* 33
casualty figures for, 36, 74, 80
enthusiasm of, 19
leadership of, 21
supplies for, 71, 72
at war's end, 78, 83
See also soldiers
Confederate Navy, 48, 49
Confederate States of America, 15
advantages of, 21
flag of, 19, 78
president of, 19
resources of, 74
See also South, the; Confederate Army

Cook, George, 25
cotton industry, in the South, 12, *12*

Davis, Jefferson, 19
Davis, Theodore, 22
deaths. *See* casualty figures
Dictator, the, 55, *55*
"Dixie" (song), 21, 47
Douglass, Frederick, 52, *82*
drilling, of soldiers, 40, *40*
drummer boys, 32–33, *33*

Economy
    of the North, 12, 71, 72
    of the South, 11, 12, 14
Emancipation Proclamation, 51, *51*, 52
enlistment
    of African Americans, 52
    of Union soldiers, 18
equipment, 54
    See also artillery; railroad; telegraph; ironclad
      ships

Factories, and war supplies, *10, 11*, 20, 71
family relationships, during war, 16, 32, 46
Farragut, David G., 49, *49*
Five Forks, Battle of, 76, *76*
food, and camp life, 41, 43
Forbes, Edwin, 22
Fort Fisher, North Carolina, 76, *76*
Fort Sumter, South Carolina, 15, 18
Fort Wagner, Battle of, 53, *53*
friendships, and Civil War, 16, 46, 47

Gambling, and camp life, 45, *45*
Gardner, Alexander, 25, 55, 69
Georgia, Sherman's march through, 75, *75*
Gettysburg, Battle of, *67*, 67–70, *68, 69*
Gettysburg Address, 70, *70*
Gibbons, James Sloan, 18
Gilmore, Patrick Sarsfield, 79
Grant, Ulysses S., 66, *66*, 71, 73, *73*, 74, 78, *78*
Greenhow, Rose O'Neil, 65, *65*

Holmes, Oliver Wendell, 15
Holmes, Oliver Wendell, Jr., 31
Homer, Winslow, 22

Infantry charge, 56
ironclad ships, 48, *48*, 49, *49*, 58, *58*

Jackson, Mississippi, 77
Jackson, Thomas "Stonewall," 35

Kittredge, Walter, 46

Lathrop, George Parsons, 68
Lee, Robert E., 17, *21*
    at Antietam, 50
    at Battle of the Wilderness, 74
    at Five Forks, 76
    at Gettysburg, 68, 69
    as military strategist, 21
    and surrender at Appomattox, 78, *78*
Liberator, The, 14
Lincoln, Abraham, 14, *15*, 48, *80, 81*, 85
    at Antietam, 51, *51*

assassination of, 81
election of, 15
and Emancipation Proclamation, 51
and Gettysburg Address, 70, *70*
and Ulysses S. Grant, 73
Lincoln, Mrs. Abraham, 16

McCarthy, Harry, 19
McClellan, George, 50, 51
Manassas Junction, Virginia, 34, 37
manufacturing capabilities
    of the North, *10, 11*, 20, 71
    of the South, 20
Massachusetts 54th Regiment, 53, *53*
Meade, George G., 68
medical treatment, during war, 62, 63, 64
Merrimac, 48, *48*
military strategy
    and modern warfare, 56, 59
    and Robert E. Lee, 21
    and Sherman's march to the sea, 75
Monitor, 48, *48*
monuments, and memorials to soldiers, 83
music. *See* songs

Nashville, 49
Nast, Thomas, 22
naval blockade
    of the South, 48, 49, 50, 76
    of Vicksburg, Mississippi, 66
naval warfare, 58
    See also ironclad ships

North, the
  factories in, *10*, *11*, 20
  resources and population of, 20, 21, 71, 72
  shipbuilding capabilities of, 49
  See also Union Army

Observation balloons, 54, 59, *59*
O'Sullivan, Timothy, 25

Patriotism
  and age of soldiers, 32
  and enlistment, 18
  and songs, 18, 19, 21, 47
  of Southern soldiers, 19, 21, 78
Pegram, Robert B., 49
Pemberton, John C., 66
Petersburg, Virginia, 55
photography, and Civil War, 24–29, 30, 44
Pike, Albert, 21
plantations, and Southern economy, 12, *12*
population, of North and South, 20
prisons, military, and medical treatment in, 63

Railroad, 54, 60, *60*, 61, *61*
  artillery transport on, 55
  miles of, North and South, 20
  use of, by the North, 60, *60*, 61, 68, 71
Richmond, Virginia, 77, *77*
rifles, 54, *54*, 56
Root, George Frederick, 47

Secession, of Confederate States, 15
Sherman, William Tecumseh, 20, 75, 77

Shiloh, Battle of, 83, *83*
shipbuilding, in the North, 49
ships, ironclad, 48, *48*, 49, *49*, 58, *58*
slavery
  and abolitionists, 14
  conditions of, 13, *13*
  and Emancipation Proclamation, 51
  and Southern economy, 12, *12*
  and war's end, 82
soldiers
  African American, 52, *52*, 53, *53*
  age of, 30–33
  and camp life, 41–44, *41*, *42*, *43*, *44*, 46
  and gambling, 45, *45*
  and medical treatment, 62–63, *62–63*, *64–65*
  monuments to, 83
  and photography, 24–29, *24–29*
  training of, 40, *40*
  See also Confederate Army; Union Army
songs
  of patriotism, 18, 19, 21, 47
  and thoughts of home, 46, 79
South, the
  condition of, at war's end, 77
  economy of, 10, 11
  factories in, 20
  population of, 20
  See also Confederate Army; Confederate
    States of America
spying, 65
Stowe, Harriet Beecher, 14
surrender, at Appomattox Courthouse, 78, *78*

Telegraph, 54, 59, *59*
"Tenting Tonight on the Old Camp Grounds"
  (song), 46, *46*
tents, for soldiers, 41, *41*, 42, *42*
transportation
  and battles, 38
  of cotton, 11
  of slaves, 13
  See also railroad

Uncle Tom's Cabin, 14, *14*
Union Army
  African-American soldiers in, 52, *52*, 53, *53*
  age of soldiers in, 30–33, *31*
  casualty figures for, 36, 52, 80
  Corps of Engineers in, 61
  and enlistment, 18
  leadership of, 51, 73
  supplies for, 71, *71*, 72, *72*
  at war's end, 79, *79*, 83
  See also soldiers
Union Navy, *27*
  African-American sailors in, 52
  and blockade of the South, 48, 49, 50, 76
  and modern warfare, 58
  size of, 48
  at Vicksburg, 66
United States, 8, 20
  See also North, the
United States Army, 17
  See also Union Army

Vicksburg, Battle of, 66, *66*, 69, 73

Virginia, 48, *48*

Warfare, modern, 9
and communications, 59, *59*
and military strategy, 54, 56
and ships, 54, 58, *58*
and weapons, 54–55, *54, 55,* 57, *57,* 58
and transportation, 54, 55, 60, *60,* 61, *61*
war supplies and resources, 20, 71, 72
Washington, D.C., 35, 65, 79, *79*
Waud, Alfred R., 22
weapons. *See* arms and ammunition; artillery

"We Are Coming, Father Abraham" (song), 18
"When Johnny Comes Marching Home"
(song), 79
Whitman, Walt, 17, 81
Wilderness, Battle of the, 74, *74*
women, role of, during war, 64, *64,* 65, *65*